LITTORAL

LITTORAL

Nicholas Murray

✳

DARE-GALE PRESS

First published in Great Britain by Dare-Gale Press, 2024

www.daregale.com

ISBN 9781915968098

Front cover: Crosby Beach, with 'Another Place' by Antony Gormley (detail). Photograph by Steve Heap/Shutterstock.

Font: Typeset in 10/11pt Delicato, designed by Stefan Hattenbach.

Printed in England by One Digital Brighton on GF Smith paper certified by both Cradle to Cradle and the Forest Stewardship Council. Dare-Gale Press is committed to environmentally conscious publishing.

Thus far we have come through the winter, on this bleak and blasty shore of the Irish Sea... Always a whistle and a howl — always an eddying gust through the corridors and chambers.

Nathaniel Hawthorne, 1856

The Funeral Pyre

Season of bonfires: driftwood hauled to heaps,
salt-soaked spars dancing with blue flame,
oil cakes running to black liquid in the fire,
the grey moon of a light-bulb popping.

In a wicker basket, lodged where the fire leaps,
a drowned rat is lifted on sticks and laid
on its catafalque or blazing pyre,
intestines oozing, charred fur fragments dropping.

And the raucous laughter of boys, careless ghouls,
poking the fire with their blackened poles,
dark smoke billowing, unpleasant smells

drifting into the dunes, where a walker of dogs
gesticulates, derided by these ragged sprogs,
as they abandon kicked apart, still glowing, logs.

With My Father on the Sands

We're striding out, feet on the hard flat shore.
O, pretty emblem: Papa and son!
I cannot now decide what we are talking of
but see how this late winter sun

gilds us as we walk into the breeze,
his hair streamed white, mine in disorder,
and beside us the thin streak of Mersey,
a light-buoy riding on the water

and, beyond the Wirral, the Welsh hills,
Moel Famau (in a clear light).
But this evening only slow dredgers
on the grey tide and the approach of night

as we turn back under a mauve sky
carrying our light burden of the unsaid
towards the gables of our house
that sleeps behind its privet-palisade.

I see a figure in the dark; stranger
or friend it isn't easy to discern.
He crowns a slipping sandhill,
stares like a watcher at the stern

of some great ship that leaves the port,
making the calculus of loss and gain
that exile forces: go or stay
all's changed, pleasure or pain,

in equal portions, sweet nostalgia,
yearning to be free, anger at this:
the need for rupture, urgent change,
the anguished essence of a farewell kiss

that seals the moment when we fall apart
and time takes over, grabs the wheel,
determines from now on the destined course
as moonlight glimmers like a sheet of steel.

The Scavengers

These men in long mackintoshes, drab grey-green,
combing through driftwood by the sea-edge,
their flat caps wet with drizzle and foam-flecks.

What do they find here to fill their buckets,
bits of grey metal clattering to the vessel's floor?
Detritus scanned to be traded as scrap?

Up to the dock wall they move like beaters
fanning out on a grouse moor, attentive
to the prospect, out of nothing, of something.

Shoreline

The tide far out,
a line of grey echoing a grey sky;
container ships, decks stacked with boxes,
throb with slow movement out of the port.

When a truck of coloured building blocks,
tumbled its load on the nursery floor
we found we had piled them too high.
Now, I stifle a warning shout.

Foreshore

Flotsam and jetsam poked by walking sticks;
the sinister eye of a jellyfish blinking from blown sand,
a dense rope fender-ball, tacky with black oil.

And once a drowned Thing (a porpoise someone said)
or a rotting seal, its face buried in the sand for shame
at such abandonment, such brute exposure.

The Black Lagoon

A foul and stagnant lake, unpleasantly still,
which we tried to wake with hurled stones.

On its surface rotten timbers floated,
broken pallets, bottles, plastic sacks

that fluttered in the wind or rose
like woken sleepers to start fear

in us prowlers and pokers at its edge,
who didn't dare to try its depths.

Shrimpers

Hard to believe now, men came with wide nets
propped on the handlebars of ancient bikes.
What did they pick from that soiled sea?

Long gone, like the Swiss pastry chef
two doors down from the sweetshop
("Pots of tea for the shore") whose *baba au rhums*

were a birthday treat, succulent ooze,
of syrupy texture topped by cream
and that pert little cherry placed on top.

Leviathan

The largest dredger in the world.
We gathered to the window
watching its last voyage,
steaming to Hamburg and to scrap.

You will say that Marilyn Monroe
dead from an overdose,
or Mandela jailed, were larger things
that August 1962 when we watched it go,

but we lined up, respectful mourners,
as it slowly (majestic beast)
slipped past into a future
as black-and-white museum piece.

Boudin at Deauville

Not ours this stretch of sand: the shellfish gatherers' carts,
obedient horses in their traces, crowds trying the sea air,
and a cluster of taut sails converging under vast clouds.

Another canvas has a blown party in frock coats,
billowing black skirts, huddled survivors on a raft.
Yet another: closing tight ranks by the bathing huts,

seated on stout chairs, parasols and dogs — not quite ready,
I think, to strip to the buff for the waves, the excitement
of buffeting, knocked sideways with a whoop of laughter.

Today I am alone on our windy *plage*, except for a dog
dragging its leash, leaping, circling, mad with delight.
Then its owner glimpsed in the distance, waving madly.

The Medal

se non è vero è ben trovato

Between the barracks and the golf-course,
this trim yet angry military man is on the shore,
pacing the sand, looking out to sea.

From his hand the ribboned medal
launches a high yet falling arc
into the Mersey's unforgiving grey.

Monsignor

The priest strides out towards the sea
which lies at the street's end,
where the old road's cobbles
sink into sand like a meal-scoop.

His dog's ahead, tail wagging,
and he needs, by God, this walk
(obese and rubicund, his shiny cloth
black as a mourner's rig).

This morning I served his Mass,
mumbled the Latin to an empty church,
parted from him at the sacristy door,
eager to rip off my buttonless gear,

dump it in the walk-in cupboard,
surplice ditto in spite of its crispness,
ironed with love by the Sisters of Mary
with their sweet, disapproving looks.

Day Trippers

Out from the city on summer Sundays,
pitching tentless camp among the dunes.
Spikes of marram grass jabbed bare arms
of children surfing streams of sliding sand.

Sandwiches and pop: Dandelion and Burdock,
Cream Soda, bottles we later gathered
to collect the deposit from the little shop
whose owner eyed us with a cool suspicion.

Mouth

Heaving down the wooden slipway,
hauling our lumpish craft,
sea scouts in our navy jerseys,
grip the gunwale fore and aft.

Past us men in vivid nylon,
pulling dinghies with one hand
mock our ancient heavy vessel
slow on sea and slow on land.

Skip commands us as we slither
into Altmouth's turbid flow
where it joins the larger river,
where the throbbing coasters go.

Launched, we sit like dumb day-trippers,
hauling on a heavy sheet;
mocking racers quickly pass us,
fancy plimsolls on their feet.

In the clubhouse, freshly showered,
they'll console with fizzy drinks;
well done lads, the wind was wicked
blowing hard across the links.

Undeceived, we mount our cycles
dreaming of an Enterprise,
light and trim it rides the water —
like a skimming gull it flies.

Cnut

Place me here where I can illustrate my power,
that petty doubt, complicit moon, would try.
I am a king; I rule with that enormous "I"
before which even princes learn to cower,

seeing the kingdoms I command like these:
the rhythmic waves that make a rising tide,
that soon shall learn that no one yet defied
my mastery of people, land and seas.

Put out my chair, its splayed legs strong
in all this glistening sand; watch how
I stand defiant like a warrior in the prow
who greets his enemy with martial song.

I am autarch, lord, high ruler of the sea:
watch how the waters start to turn and flee

ii

My loyal courtiers come and gently seize
four corners of this gilded, mobile throne.
As from the dog's tight jaws you draw a bone,
they deftly pluck and lift, against my pleas,

their monarch whom they wish to save
from mockery, the people's silent stare
that says: who but a crowned buffoon would dare
to stand against the laws of nature? Brave

in being foolish, wise only in his ways
of crushing those beneath: might is right
the silent whisper in his sleep at night,
that struggles to convince in waking days.

I see that I am wrong; there is no King but He
who makes the waves, the cold, unyielding sea.

Another Place

How did they get here? In the stealthy night?
Rust-brown, soon sinking in the sand,
eyes turned, of course, towards the sea:
the tribe of Gormley's men, bolt upright

and objects of inspection to the dogs,
small boys, and those defecating gulls
who settle on their iron skulls,
with yellow feet, appointed guardians of the beach.

We are famous now, the tourists come,
picking their way across loose sand
to learn again the limpid truth that art
transforms by being here. Unfussy theorem.